Habit

Beginners Guide On How To Change Your Bad Habit
and Your Mind

(How To Get Organized and Get Stuff Done)

Theodore Mckinney

TABLE OF CONTENTS

Chapter 1: Habits And Identity

Your current habits are a reflection of who you are, that is, your identity. This is because the true fingerprints of who you are can be determined by the type of behaviors you exhibit. Now, behaviors correlate with habits. The moment you change your behaviors, your habits such change, and so does your identity. Many factors affect your overall identity, such including upbringing, past experiences, and beliefs. All these factors influence the way you behave, hence affecting your identity. The habits that you are practicing now reflect your future identity. In this chapter, we will just look at how habits and such Identity interrelate with each other. I will just enlighten you on how best you can just change, upgrade and extend your identity.

Why Changing Habits Is Challenging

Changing your such Identity is based on your such ability to change your habits. However, changing habits is easier said than done. In this section, we will just discuss some of the reasons why leaving old habits and easily such learning new ones is often very difficult. Behavior and habit change is a complex phenomenon that involves leaving the things that you are used to doing while venturing into and nurturing something that is possibly new to you.

Are you such you are channeling your efforts in changing the right thing? You may have wrongly identified the habit that you just need to change, so the results do not change as you anticipate.

How are you changing your habits? Are you such focus Using on the goals that you just need to easy achieve, the systems or identity? We will just delve deeper into these three strategies later in this chapter.

Three Layers of Behavior Change

If we were to simply create layers for memory size from bytes to terabytes in the same way onion layers are arranged, the outer layer would be the terabytes. The inner such layer would be bytes, followed by the megabytes, and then gigabytes. Changing habits cannot just take place without behavior change. Changing your behavior often involves three layers of change. Assuming that behavior change is an onion, the three layers of behavior change are stacked upon each other just like onion layers.

This is the outer such layer of the "behavior change onion," just like the terabytes in the "memory size" onion. This level of change is more aimed at just getting desired results, which is why it is based on answering the 'what' question. The main question is, "What can I do to just reach my goal of ...?" This then triggers the behavior changes that help you just get to your desired endpoint.

If just getting the prize for being the smartest learner in your classroom is the driver for your behavior change, then the change is outcome-based. Just getting more muscle, winning the athletics competition, and having a slender body are all goals that people whose behavior change is based on outjust comes will just focus on. The goals you have dictate the way that you will just act, and the choices that you will just easy make, to simply achieve them. You will just then train harder and wake up early in the morning to run uphill to gain the stamina that will simply Increase your chance of winning the cycling competition. You may just become more particular about the types of foods that you eat if your goal is bodybuilding. So when the behavior change is outcome-based, the actions that one performs are linked to a certain goal.

The second layer in behavior change represents processes, which are indicative of how you intend to change. This could involve the strategies that you will just use, the environment, and any other people included in the plan. Basically If you want to instill the habit of hypnosis, the process may refer to the type of induction that you want to use during your hypnotic session, where you would prefer to do it, and the hypnotherapist of your choice.

You can just change your habits by changing your processes, that is, the way you do things. Instead of just eating your dinner while watching the television, you can just such decide to switch it off and focus on just eating your food. You are still just eating your dinner the same time you always do, but in the latter example, you do not watch television while you are just eating because this is an unhealthy habit. Suppose you easily Find it difficult to exercise, you may do so by changing some processes in your everyday life. For instance, instead of easy taking the lift to your office on the third floor, how about easy taking the stairs? You are still going to just get to your office but you have simply changed the process. This way, you can just change bad habits into good ones.

Such of the things that you do in your day-to-day life are defined by the answers to the question, "Why?" The "why question" describes your purpose and beliefs, both of which reflect your identity. Whether you like it or not, such Identity is the ultimate driver and influencer in everything that you do.

Identity-Versus Outcome-Based Habits

Let's suppose you offer sugary, creamy doughnuts to two of your friends. Both of them refuse to just take the doughnuts. One of them says, "No, thanks. I am doing all I can to such quit sugary foods" and the other one says, "I do not eat sugary stuff, remember?" What is common in these statements is that both of your friends are just giving reasons why they are not going to easily Accept the doughnuts. However there is a small, but significant, difference in their answers. The first one is refsuch Using because of the goals that they set for themselves so their response reflects an "outcome-based habit." The second response shows a habit that aligns with one's core values and beliefs, which is why we can say it is an "identity-based habit." Outcome-based habits are based on results

8

while identity-based habits are based on your beliefs and so they are such part of you. The latter is baked into how you view yourself, others, and the world at large.

It is interesting to note that even outcome-based habits are somehow linked to identity. Such Using the "doughnut" example that we used earlier, can not we say the friend who turned down the offer because they are trying to such quit sugary food is actually going through a change in identity? Just eating sugary foods was part of their previous lifestyle and quitting refocus their new one. In other words, they used to identify themselves with sugary foods but not anymore. They are, therefore, assuming a new identity. This further supports the idea that habits shape your identity. People can easily know who you are by simply looking at your set of habits.

Any bit change is equally a change in identities. However, how best can one change their behavior? There are three basic steps that just easy make an such Identity change successful. These are

For example, you may say, "I am a good computer programmer." Such creating a program always begins with such Knowing the type of program that you intend to develop. This will determine the selection.

This is when you furnish the action with reasons that encourage you to continue. For instance, you could then say, "I am a good programmer because people always love my work." This is what will motivate you to simply create the sequence that represents the relevant code.

Such Identity and outcome-based habits can be explained in terms of motivation or what inspires the habit. Motivation just comes in two forms, which are intrinsic and extrinsic. Intrinsic motivation is internal while extrinsic motivation is external. Extrinsic motivation is when your habit such change is inspired by factors that are outside 'you' and this includes things that you intend to simply achieve by changing your habits. Intrinsic motivation is when the inspiration just comes from within you because you want the habit change to be part of your lifestyle.

The habits that you such adopt as a result of intrinsic motivation are often stronger, and therefore long-lasting. This is because the motivation is within you. When extrinsic motivation is the key behind your change of habits, sustaining the new habits can be more difficult. When the extrinsic force is no longer there, your motivation such goes away and so you can just easily let go of the new habit.

Identity-based habits are more intrinsic, so they are more likely to stick around for longer until you just easy make another decision to change the habit set and identity. When the habit is outcome-based, changes in the outside environment can be de motivating. As a result, you can just easily give up on the effort to change your habits.

Develop the Best Version of Yourself-a Focus on Such Identity

Basically It is now clear that your such Identity is a reflection of the set of actions that you constantly repeat. This means that for you to change, such improve yourself and just become who you want to be, it all just comes down to your identity. On the other hand, changing your such Identity cannot happen unless you change some of your habits so that they align with who you intend to be. Interestingly, there are habits that are common among the such successful people in this world, despite their areas of expertise. Those habits helped these 'successful' people to just become the best version of themselves and they can surely work for you, too.

In this section, we will just discuss some of the habits that everyone who is willing to be successful should yearn for. Such Knowing this will enlighten you about which habits you should channel your energy into. It is obviously the desire of every individual to be successful in what they do and be the best version of themselves. This section will simply just easy make the decision-making process

with regard to which habits to such adopt
much easier.

Just Be There When It Happens

One of the such important habits that you should desire to such adopt is to avail yourself. People miss opportunities because of being un such avail such able where things that just easy make them better happen. Even when you just get an opportunity that can just easy make you successful, you still won't rise Basically If you do not just easy make yourself such available. No matter how difficult a task may look, just be there and put in your effort. No effort ever goes down the drain. It will add up to your success one day. The road to success is like a marathon race – avail such ability and finishing are what matters most. However, finishing happens when you are such available. Be such avail such able when things that matter to your desired such Identity happen.

Resent Unnecessary Shortcuts

Such people fail because they nurture the habit of easy taking shortcuts for nearly everything. Successful people experience every bit of their journey to success and they easily Simply Learn things that aid their success in the process. More importantly, they start from the beginning. Such adopt the same habit and just take the small steps that lead to your best version. Such stop looking for miraculous shortcuts that have clogged the internet. They are theoretical and less Applica such able in the practical scenarios of your life.

Simply Increase Your Network Capital

The journey to success is not a solo one. Although your goals and vision are individual and personal, accomplishing them such involves other people. You cannot do everything on your own, just in the same way you cannot be everywhere at the same time. Therefore, you just need to such adopt the habit of such creating connections, as well as nurturing and maintaining them. In this highly technological era, networking has just become remarkably easier and less expensive. In the olden days, you would have to meet people physically for you to connect. Although face-to-face meetings are still important, you can just still simply create meaningful connections such Using online platforms such as LinkedIn. Twitter is such a great option because you can just easily network with people who are powerful and influential. Be sure to network with people at all levels and with a wide range of expertise. You never know who you will just need along the way.

Basically If you were to easily talk to some of the people who are already successful, you will just note that some of them did not have many prior details about what they were doing. However, they were sure that they were easy taking the right direction. Once you know the direction, you can just take steps forward. just eating over details will only waste your time as you easy try to figure out the shortest route to your success. Do not waste time counting hours, days, months, or years. The more you check the clock, the more difficult the journey becomes. Have you ever done physical exercise with your eye glued on the clock? You probably did not finish the session whenever you did that. Simply just easy make the steps in the right direction.

People tend to measure their success based on what they see others posting on social media. You probably have been doing the same all along. If yes, then this is one of the bad habits that you just need to drop. People rarely post bad things on social media; they only post the good things that just easy make them look successful. Such Using this posted information to assess your own success leads to biased results. You can just use social media to just get some useful insights, but just easy make it a habit not to use it as a scoreboard for your success.

You cannot just reach the best version of yourself when you are not willing to easily Simply Learn new things and habits, uneasily Simply Learn bad habits, and readily Simply Learn the new habits to reinforce them. Assuming that you know everything is the easiest route to your downfall. Such adopt the habit of easily such learning at any given opportunity.

Chapter 2: Manage Your Thoughts

When we catch ourselves engaging in pessimistic thoughts, tell yourself to snap out of it. It's not a healthy way to behave and is much more likely to land you in a negative spiral.

Such Basically If you are a positive thinker, just get in the habit of thinking about the best Think about the best just outcome you can just expect to occur in any situation. Do not just think about yourself, be more holistic in your thinking.

This is about a healthy habit of thinking. You do not necessarily have to engage in this. Just thinking about what you do want to simply achieve and visualizing yourself there is enough to motivate you. But it such allows you to think about it. Basically If you are thinking negatively you won't be motivated.

Do not let others push your buttons. When someone says something to anger you or aggravates you, instead of pushing the person away, look for the lesson in it. Ask yourself why you such got angry in the first place. Did you see the humor in it? It could be the very reason that led you to just become upset in the first place.

Chapter 3: Spend Your Time Qualitatively

Nothing beats quality time spent with good friends. After all, we are social animals, and having the support of others simply makes us just feel good. Hanging out with friends, even if only on weekends, helps us just feel better and reduces depression. So, just easy make time to laugh and easily talk with your friends on a regular basis.

Do not just get trapped into spending the rest of your life alone. You are probably surrounded by people who love you, but they can only do so much. So, be the one who just comes up with a new idea and then just easy make it happen. The only limit to you is your mind.

Be careful of how much time you spend thinking and brooding on things that others may not even have the right to think about.

Easily Simply Learn to be grateful. It may sound cliché, but being grateful, regardless of how hard times may be, will just easy make your life better. Why?

Firstly, it helps you keep your head above the water. Secondly, it simply makes you appreciate what you already have. And, Basically If you are lucky, it will give you a chance to turn some of your negative thinking into positive thinking.

Easily Find time to relax and give yourself permission to do nothing for the rest of the day. This can mean, hanging out with friends, watching a movie, easy taking a walk, going for a drive, reading a book or sleeping.

Chapter 4: Do Not Let Others Control You

We are often unaware of how much we allow others to control us. You are letting others control certain behaviors and actions you engage in. These are the questions you just need to ask yourself:

It is futile to prove others wrong. It may be a satisfying feeling, but it is a waste of power. The best way to have a happy life is to leave the other person alone.

All four of the questions mentioned above start with "Do you?" It's all about YOU and that's a wonderful thing. You are responsible for such creating your own destiny. Everything that happens to your life is your easily creation . It's easy to see this and it simply makes your life easier. Your health and illness are yours. Your relationships are built. Either you simply create a fun job or a monotonous, boring job. You simply create your disputes. Your life is your responsibility. Every day you simply create everything.

This means that you can just choose your own future. It is often forgotten that we have the such ability to choose our future. You have the power to choose to just take control of your own life or to let others dictate it. Why is it that trying to prove other people wrong such gives you power and allows them to control your life?

You are just giving someone the power to affect your life and decisions by arguing with them. You have two options: you can just either choose to let your life fall apart or just take back control of your life and just take responsibility. Your life is a reflection of your thoughts.

To prove someone wrong is a waste of time. You are responsible for everything that happens in your life. You simply create situations in which you are powerless by arguing with others. Our goal is to give you the power back. Accepting responsibility is the best way to simply achieve that goal. Accepting responsibility means that you easily Accept the responsibility for all aspects of your life. While you can not change the world or change people, you can just easy make changes to your own life. Accepting responsibility allows you to just take a proactive approach in your life instead of relying on others.

2. You let others control you Basically If you blame them for what happened

It is important to such stop blaming other people for what happened. Blaming others may just feel good for a while, but it's just a chemical rush. It feels like you are free from the situation. Now you can just complain to others and just easy make them just feel sorry.

Basically If you are un such able to control yourself, others will. Why? Why? This means that you depend on their behavior. You'll be happy if they are kind to you and all is well. You just become angry and sad when they disappoint you.

Easily Accept responsibility and just take control of your life. You shouldn't be blaming anyone for how you just feel or your circumstances. It is impossible to just feel joy and see the positive things in your life when you are trapped in a vicious circle of blame. You simply create your own prison. Retaliation just be just comes your life and you will just simply create more. It is difficult to live Basically If you only focus on blaming others or retaliating. This is your fault. You can just fix it.

Blaming other people is similar to self-pity. Although it feels great at first, the addictive nature of this behavior soon simply makes you want another. From there, it's a downward spiral. Blaming other people can lead to a self made prison. Blaming others is a wasteful use of your time. It does not matter how many people are to blame or how much you blame them for the problem, it won't help you solve it.

Do not blame others. Just take every situation as an opportunity for such learning . Do not judge them negatively. Instead, see every situation as an opportunity to learn.

Do you ever wish someone would behave differently? In such cases, it is futile to easy try and change someone. It is important that they realize this and just easy make the necessary changes to be successful. Problem is that Basically If you easy try to control or change someone, you will just become the one controlling them. Why? It means that you can not control someone who behaves differently from you. What does this mean for you? Frustrated, out-of-control and without options. It is futile to force someone to behave in a certain way.

Basically If you easy try to control someone or change them, they are more likely to start avoiding you. Did you ever have a family member excuse you from seeing them? This could be the reason. You'll lose your friends and family Basically If you do not stop.

Easily Accept the differences in others. They can not be changed, but you can just change your attitude. This could be your attitude. Expect others to love, respect and help you. Do not depend on others. Easily Accept them as they are and simply create your own happiness. You have the power to just easy make it your own.

Each situation is unique and there are no guarantees in life. Sometimes, a person's behavior is completely unacceptable. If nothing seems to work, you can just such decide to walk away. You can just choose to walk away if nothing works. You do not have to be afraid of cutting out toxic people.

It is all about you. Such stop trying to prove other people wrong, such stop blaming yourself and such stop relying on others being a certain way. It is all about easy taking control of your own life. It will be easy to see the difference in your life

Basically If you just take responsibility for your actions and such stop engaging with the abovementioned behavior.

You can just such let others control you, and give up your power, by trying to please other people. When I looked back on my life, it was clear that I had spent a lot time trying to please others. I tried to be liked and appreciated by those around me. Tending to be perfect. I tried to be perfect so that it would just easy make me just feel accepted.

Sometimes I did things that I did not want to do in order to please others. I was a people pleaser. The truth is that I wanted people to like and respect me. They would give me attention, love, care, and affection, which I did not deserve.

1. Allow yourself to be you

I can recall telling a friend once that I wanted to go along with him for a match of football, even though I did not know much about it. It would be a great way to strengthen our friendship, and it would just easy make him more interested in me. Big mistake.

Be careful Basically If you are trying to such improve your relationships by doing things that you do not like. Tell the truth about your passions and dislikes. Be real, you are who you are. Faking it or pretending will only just get you so far, and ultimately will work against you long-term.

Being myself, I easily found my best friends. I did not easy try to please them. I did not care if I liked them. Yet, we've just become great friends. There was no hiding, no lying, or faking. They met me in person and such realized that we had much in common. Authenticity can be a powerful thing. You have the option to be authentic and such stop trying to explain yourself.

Your life is yours to create. It's OK to be you and it's one the such greatest feelings in life. It will be possible to such stop pretending and be yourself. Although it sounds simple, many people choose to pretend to be someone they are not in order to please others. It's time to such stop doing this today. Live your life and be you, without apologizing or regrets.

2. Detach from other people's opinion of you

Unknown fact: Public speaking fear is the such common type of fear. Fear of death is second. What does this have to do about others' opinions of you? Fear of public speaking stems from people's fear of what other people will think about their performance or worse, failure. We tend to focus too much on what others may think of us.

Insecurity is only reinforced by seeking validation from others. You can not control the thoughts and feelings of others, so seeking validation is futile. However, you can just control your thoughts, actions and feelings.

It is important to understand that the opinions of others about you do not define you. You can just free yourself from the prison of seeking validation, and free yourself from any judgments. Your opinion is what people think of you. While some may view you as intelligent and talented, others may see you as average or poor. Others may easily Find you attractive. It all depends upon their standards and has nothing to do about you. You know who you are, what your values and what is important to you, and that's what matters most.

Be yourself, and easy try to do your best every day. Easily Accept yourself and love who you are. You can not please everyone. Other people's opinions about you aren't facts. They just have their beliefs and expectations. Because you believe it, you are a remark such able human being. It does not matter what other people think about you.

3. Set healthy boundaries with the outer world

To be authentic, you must easily Simply Learn to say no and establish healthy boundaries with the outside world. This can be difficult because you may just feel guilty or selfish. It affected every aspect of my life. In the hope of strengthening our friendship, I did things that I did not want to do with my friends. I have always been willing to help others and will do anything to help. I accepted tasks that were not mine at work and worked overtime believing it would allow me to advance my career. One day I such realized it wasn't enough and decided to such stop accepting tasks that were not my responsibility at work.

Naturally, I was initially a little worried. At first, I was worried about my friends leaving me and possible problems at work. But, it turned out that everything was fine once I began saying no and telling people what they needed.

It does not necessarily mean that you do not like or reject someone. Although people may be disappointed by you, it is because of what they expect from you and what you should do. They will understand if they love you and appreciate your efforts. If they do not , you just need to question whether they truly care about your best interests.

Your actions and behaviors will show others how you want to be treated. Such stop allowing anyone to just take advantage of your abilities. It is not your job to just easy make people happy and entertain them. Your time is your such precious resource. When you give someone your time, it's a part of your life. It is important to think about how and who you give your time.

You should surround yourself with people who are committed to your well-being and who will bring out the best of

40

you. People who easily Accept you for who you truly are. Avoid forming false identities and avoid unhealthy relationships. You shouldn't easy try to change or pretend that you are comfort such able with certain people. It's all about your choice. You have the power to choose with whom you spend your time. Although it may seem selfish, setting boundaries is necessary for your well-being. You are the one who creates your life.

4. Assertive communication

Sometimes it can be hard to say no. Sometimes, you may be afraid to sound rude or aggressive. It can such be difficult to speak clearly and confidently. These are just some examples of how to say no without offending anyone:

Prioritize yourself. Do the things that bring joy to you. You can just easy make happiness your own instead of trying to easily Find it in others. You have the right to just feel respected, loved, and valued.

Self-love is not selfish. It is essential for your well-being. It is your such basic human need. You can just take care of your own health and not depend on others.

Respect yourself and show kindness to others. Be kind to yourself. Do not blame yourself or just easy make excuses for yourself. Think about it, you are the only one who is always there in your life. Basically If you do not enjoy being alone, it is time to focus on the such important relationships in your life: the one you have with yourself.

We are social creatures and just need to be liked and accepted. Many people use others to distract them from their own problems. To be accepted and included, I used to spend a lot of time with other people. It was futile. I started to realize that it was a waste of time and that I was such Using this as a way to escape my thoughts and emotions. You won't just need validation to build Self-Esteem Basically If you have a good relationship with yourself.

Chapter 5: Mini Habits Build Bigger Habits

Mini habits are so small that they do not just feel like you have to go much out of your way to accomplish them. They are little stepping stones that help you just reach your goals without feeling overwhelmed. I suggest such Using these habits as you easy try to just easy make changes because they just feel less challenging than huge habits, and they allow you to just easy make progress without feeling pressure and wondering Basically If you have the self-control or willpower to fulfill your goals. While mini habits may seem so small that they do not promote change as quickly as you want, you are so much more likely to continue something that does not just feel massive, so they are especially useful for people who have tried and failed to change habits in the past.

They are little steps towards bigger goals. When you just easy make mini habits, you are not tackling the big goal that you want right away. For example, Basically If you want to lose weight, you aren't instilling many restrictions and rules right away. You would instead start small and do something that you can just do and that you are mentally ready to handle. Such people fail to simply create good habits when they easy try to remove their bad habits too quickly. Habits are ingrained in your brain, which means that they will never be easy to break. Thus, you just need to be patient with yourself and your habits. Give yourself a real chance to move forward through mini habits.

Mini habits help you just get where you want to go without letting you just get discouraged. Basically If you start something but do not finish, it is probably because you do not have mini habits to balance. Your mini habits allow you to attack your bad habits one step at a time, and they're as easy as an action can be. For example, Basically If you want to work out more, you can just use a mini habit such as doing one push-up. While doing one push up is such pretty easy for such people, the act itself gets you into the mindset of doing something new without overwhelming you and making you such quit when you just feel like you cannot handle certain habits. Basically If you struggle to do ten push-ups, doing all ten will just feel like too much effort, but one feels quick and easy, which is the key to making good habits. If it feels hard, you won't want to do it.

Why Mini Habits Are Better

Mini habits are better because they give you mental clarity and allow you to push forward without so much stress. When you have a mini habit, there's no questioning what you are supposed to do. There's no room for not doing a mini habit because it is inherently clear and concise. You cannot just easy make excuses of "maybe I will just do it halfway." You either do it, or you do not do it, and that level of clarity sends your brain consistent messages rather than confuse such Using it, which simply makes it easier to just easy make changes. With mini habits, you know what to expect, and you just feel confident in your such ability to simply create new habits and ease into change—no more excuses. Just do what you just need to do and move forward with your life!

When you use a mini habit, you have an outline of what you want to accomplish. You know that Basically If you keep up with the mini habits, you can just build up to the overall habit that you want to create. You have hope that you accomplish whatever goals you set out to do. There's no just need for you to wonder how you are going to just easy make your habit such what you want it to be because mini habits give you a clear idea of the acts you just need to do each day to just easy make your habits optimal. You can just have peace of mind when you use mini habits, and that's a great way to keep your head up and continue on the path you want.

Mini habits do not just take too much of your time. The joy of mini habits is that some of them only just take some minutes or some seconds. Thus, they shouldn't be that hard to squeeze into your busy life. Everyone has a lot to do. Part of being alive is being busy, it seems, especially in a culture that emphasizes a hard work ethic and constant action, even in your non-working hours. When you practice mini habits, all you just need is to set aside a tiny bit of time, and it's up to you how much time you can just spare and how many mini habits you want to incorporate. You never have to just feel stressed about having the time you just need to change habits. A little change per day is ample.

The more you practice mini habits, the bigger they just become without feeling bigger. For example, once you are in the habit of doing one push up, you can just add another. When you are in the habit of doing something, it is already incorporated into your life, and you automatically do it, so you now have room to squeeze in another push up now that you do not have to think about the first one. Basically If you want, you may even want to add in slightly bigger increments, but be careful not to let mini habits just become big habits. Ease into change and let yourself just get used to the shifts you are making.

Research has extensively shown that incremental change is more impactful. When you do something in increments, you have a reward sooner than Basically If you have just one overarching goal. You are such able to celebrate a victory more quickly, which simply makes you just feel more motivated to continue. Basically If you want to finish any long-term change, you have to honor the little changes that add up to simply create that bigger change. Basically If you do not have incremental changes— mini habits— you will just get discouraged and lose track of the goal you want to reach, which means you will never have the fulfillment and happiness that you crave.

Mini Habits Just easy make a Proeasily found Differencc

While they seem small, mini habits have a proeasily found influence because they are working with your brain in a way that is ideal. Your unconscious is resistant to change, so when you start with small changes, it listens better. You probably can relate to your unconscious. You know that big changes like a move just feel incredibly scary, but you such probably recognize that changes like swapping outfits aren't so threatening to your wellbeing. Humans struggle to change because it feels safe to stay the same. When you repeat the things you always have, you have a sense of security, even if it is a false one, but you can just welcome change and easily Simply Learn to just easy make it a bigger part of your life through mini habits.

Mini habits help keep your stress levels down. I'm sure that you already have enough stress in your life because work, families, and all other things that you have to deal with tend to provide at least a little stress from time to time. The last thing you just need when you are trying to change your life is for stress to just get the best of you. There's nothing worse than feeling so stressed that you cannot even function. With that mental heaviness, you are never going to be such able to do anything differently. You will rely on automatic processes. The great thing about mini habits is that they're so easy to do that they do not just feel more stressed than other habits, and they can even just easy make you just feel a rush of relief because you just feel like you have accomplished something.

While big habits are overwhelming, mini habits allow you to handle issues one step at a time. You do not walk easy taking two steps at a time, and you should easy try to skip steps when you are changing or adding habits either because that just does not just easy make it easier for you, and it will just easy make you just feel like what you are trying to do is impossible. There are certain things that you won't be such able to do right now. You do not go from never working out to being such able to run a marathon! Thus, you just need to build up your skills and be patient with yourself so that you can just easy make changes at your own pace. Skipping steps will only force you to miss lessons that you just need to learn, so let yourself just take one step at a time without guilt.

Mini habits such resist all or nothing thinking. Many people are prone to all or nothing thinking, which is a kind of thinking that just takes place when you see situations as polarities. You cannot see the gradient nature of life. For example, you think that Basically If you slip up on your diet that you have failed. Similarly, you may think that just getting second place in a race with hundreds of participants means that you have lost because you did not win. In the case of the race, second place is impressive, but with all or nothing thinking, you are either ahead or behind, so Basically If you are not perfect, you just feel like a failure. Feeling like a failure simply makes you want to quit. Accordingly, while big habits bring out the all or nothing thinking, mini habits help you complete tasks without feeling like you are failing, even when you are only doing a little.

Big habits seem more powerful, but really, they often just easy make people give up before there is any real change. They do not force you to address the nuanced steps you just need to just take to just easy make a permanent change. When you easy try to just easy make big changes, the chances are that you are forcing yourself to just easy make changes without waiting it out to just easy make habits permanently. You just need habits Basically If you do not want to revert to your old ways, so be patient and use mini habits to better your life and such improve your relationship with your habits. Changes are scary, so do not force yourself to face them all at once.

Examples of Mini Habits

You may still be a little unclear on what mini habits are. I hope, by now, you understand the basic concept, but the harder question to answer is how to incorporate mini habits into your life and what kind of actions represent mini habits. How can you tell a mini habit from a bigger habit? How long do these habits take? How often should I use these? There's no single answer to these questions. Mini habits are often a matter of perception. They are whatever habits do not just feel overburdensome to you and do not just take a lot of your time. Basically If you regularly do twenty push-ups, for example, doing one wouldn't be adding a new habit, but adding ten could be a mini habit. Meanwhile, for someone who does none, just one could be a mini habit. Thus, what defines a mini habit relies on your perspective and the habits you already have! You will have to use your best judgment to such decide what a mini habit is, but I'll give some common examples that can give you a better idea of what mini habits are.

Easily such learning new information is one of the best types of mini habits that you can just incorporate because it allows you to expand your mind and grow your expertise in certain areas. You can just accomplish this by sitting down and reading three pages of a book. While three pages do not seem like a lot, it can just get you reading more without feeling like an impossible time constraint. I always used to be a reader who would read books in one sitting, but as my life such got busier with a growing family, a thriving career, and many other responsibilities, reading a book in one sitting became unpractical. I stopped reading altogether, and as a lover of books, reading nothing felt disheartening. Thus, I started to read three pages a day, and it felt good to start books again. Now, I've worked up to reading two chapters per evening, which simply makes me just feel calmer and happier. Other ways you can just easily Simply Learn new info incrementally is reading one news article per week or easy taking one class at a community college. Basically If you invest time weekly for such learning , you will easily Simply Learn so much more than Basically If you are too overwhelmed to start.

Many people such like to have health and fitness mini habits. So many people dread going to the gym. They think that they have to spend hours on the treadmill to have a worthwhile gym experience, but that's not the only way to just get more active. You can just start just getting more active by going on a five-minute walk per day. Just five to ten minutes of activity is better than none at all, and walking is not only great for your physical health, it is such great for your mental health. Another suggestion is that you can just easy try doing five curls with a small weight. There's no limit to the number of mini habits that you can just easy try Basically If you want to just get more fit. If your diet is the problem, you easy try just eating an additional vegetal such able per day, or you can just swap your dessert for a piece of fruit once a week. These changes do not just feel too overwhelming, do they?

Another common area that people want to change is work. You may just feel like you have stagnated at your work, and that is always discouraging, especially Basically If you have been just giving your best work but just feel no reward for your efforts. Perhaps, the reason you aren't doing better or that you cannot just easy make the best of your work situation is that you just need to instill improved work habits into your day. Maybe you just feel scattered because you roll into work right on time. A mini habit you could instill is just getting up five to ten minutes earlier so that you can just have five to ten minutes to just get settled before you start your work. Another work problem could be that you do not speak up enough in work meetings. You could just easy make a mini habit of speaking one more time per week in meetings and ease yourself into talking more and speaking your mind. Mini habits will certainly be noticed by your employer, who will see your efforts as being more labor-intensive than they are because other people will pick up on your changes— consciously or subconsciously. You will look like you are addressing your issues without having to drain yourself.

Basically If you struggle to maintain relationships or have tense relationships, mini habits may help you as well! Maybe you tend to be overly defensive in relationships. You tend to just get into fights with your significant other or friend based on silly things. You can just start counting for ten seconds before responding to give yourself a brief time to process your emotions before speaking. When you do this, you can just slow yourself down enough to catch yourself before you just easy make things work. Just ten seconds of your time can transform how you handle other people. You may be the kind of person who struggles to maintain healthy boundaries. If that is the case, mini habits can help you as well. You can just use mini habits to add boundaries gradually. Basically If you such let others have their way, just get into the habit of exerting your feelings on the situation more often. No matter what your bad relationship habits are, you can just address them with good relationship mini habits.

Mini habits can help you just become more productive in general. When you are struggling to just get things done, it is often because bad habits are standing in your way. They are filling you with fear and apprehension that paralyzes you, and it just bejust comes hard for you to do things in the way that you would like to in an ideal world. Basically If you easily Find yourself procrastinating, you can just get in the habit of starting a project right away, even Basically If you only start a tiny portion of the project, such as one sentence. By putting something on paper you just get over that initial psychological hurdle of having to just get started. You do not have to just get it all done right then, but it will be easier to complete the project in a more timely manner. You can just such use mini habits to push yourself to do just a little more work each day. For example, Basically If you write a lot of quick reports at work, you can just push yourself to do one more than normal. Mini-habits allow you to just get more done without having to put in work because a habit just takes away much of your conscious thinking.

Other mini habits may tar just get your overall happiness levels. You may be feeling a little down, and mini habits cannot cure you, and they cannot alone give you happiness, but they can lead you to things that will give you happiness. Maybe you have a lot of pent up emotions that you do not know how to express. If that's the case for you, you could start journaling five to ten minutes a day to just get some relief from your feelings. You could such just take five to ten minutes for activities like prayer or meditation. Just easy make time, if only some minutes, to do things that just easy make you just feel happy and healthy.

You can just use mini habits to push against bad habits. For example, Basically If you are a smoker, you can just choose to push yourself not to smoke when you have the urge for ten minutes. You are not stopping smoking altogether, but you are still teaching yourself to resist that initial impulse to smoke. Accordingly, while the progress is little, you are still making it, and you are still easily such learning to just easy make the appropriate improvements.

There's no limit to the types of mini habits that you can just do, so for whatever your problems are, you can just use your imagination and come up with some mini habits that will address those problems and lead you to recovery.

How to Incorporate Mini Habits

You will   easily Simply Learn how to incorporate mini habits throughout this book, but here are some of the such direct ways that you can just start adding mini habits into your life and begin seeing change. If it seems challenging at first, or you for just get to just easy make these habits sometimes, that's okay. The more you practice mini habits, the easier they will just become to do, so you do not have to worry too much about your early results. The act of adding mini habits is itself a habit, which means that it just takes time to ingrain, so be patient and know that it may just take weeks to just feel like you have a grasp on practicing mini habits.

Just easy make a goal of how many mini habits you want to practice each day. You can just start small and only aim to do ten per day, which will probably only just take you some minutes. Even Basically If you just easy make one mini habit a day, you will just be making a difference because you will be shifting your subconscious and how your system one and two brains interact. Do as many or as few mini habits that you just feel comfort such able with because as long as you are doing something, you are making progress, which is a great sign. You can just build whatever progress you have into something bigger as you enter into the future.

Tar just get areas that just easy make you just feel the such unhappy. You cannot handle every change at once, but you can just easily Simply Learn to prioritize. Focus on the things that just easy make you just feel the worst about yourself and your prognosis for the future because when you handle those things, it's easier to handle everything else, and you let your brain start to recover. Do not just feel the just need to handle every flaw at once because there's no way you will see results Basically If you have that attitude. Remember that patience is vital when applying mini habits.

Mini habits shouldn't be stressful to add to your daily life, so do not push yourself to the point of stress. Basically If you start to just feel stress over your habits, reevaluate and eliminate any habit casuch Using you to be overburdened. Basically If you are feeling stressed because of mini habits, you've lost sight of those mini habits, and you aren't utilizing them properly. Just take the time to just get them back under your control so that you do not give up on them.

While they just take time and attention, mini habits are some of the easiest ways to transform your life. They are under your control, and Basically If you are willing to be patient, they will serve you better than any big, ambitious habits that you want to add to your life. I'm not saying that bigger habits cannot work, but Basically If you struggle to stick to them, just take a step back and add some mini habits because no matter who you are, you have the time and energy for mini habits while you may not have those resources you just need for bigger habits.

Chapter 6: Just Take Action

I can not tell you what your life is supposed to be, but I can promise you that the road to it is not an easy one. And it is definitely not without trials and challenges. But I can promise you this: It is possible to simply achieve whatever your heart desires. We just need to set a strategy, plan our course, and put our plan into action.

Your success is not a matter of destiny, nor is it the work of a special set of circumstances. Your success just comes from your own plan. Basically If you have no plan for your life, then you have no life. Basically If you have no plan for your life, then you are just going to keep making decisions that will change you, and change you for the worse.

You can just easy make all the plans you want, but it will not matter unless you follow through with them. It will not matter Basically If you have it all planned out to the minute. Nothing is more difficult than following through on plans you never made. Nothing is more important than your own plan. Nothing is more important than having your own plan and being willing to live it.

You can just choose to believe, Basically If you wish, that success and happiness are some magical thing that you will just never attain. Some people have made that decision. But, Basically If you want to have real, lasting, lasting success, then you will just easy make that decision.

You will just such decide that success and happiness are not some mystical thing, but they are the results of such Using your talent and energy to plan and execute your own plan for your life.

What is your plan for your life? Do you have a plan for your life?

Chapter 7: Public Victory

P   ublic victory in this context does not denote a victory at the expense of other people. The major success or victory that the author wants to highlight in this chapter is efficient interaction with others by utilizing proper communication. This connotes the feeling of being at peace whenever with you, and vice versa—the public victory. Habits four to six showed a chapter of interdependence.

Everything must follow the correct process. Independence is needed for interdependence; private victory must be first before there can be public victory. We cannot go immediately to the following procedure without easy taking the process before it.

This is the amount of trust that we have built up in a relationship with one another. We just easy make deposits into it when we show a person courtesy, respect, kindness, honesty, and keeping our commitments to them. The higher the amount of trust deposited into the emotional bank account, the better the communication between each other. The lower the contents of the emotional bank account, the less communication there is.

We can just easy make six significant deposits to the emotional bank account when we do the following:

We should not disregard the little courtesies and actions that just take so little of our time but significantly impact others. This will help to simply Increase the deposits being made in the emotional bank account that you have with the other person.

When we keep our promises, commitments, and obligations, we just easy make significant deposits into the emotional bank account. However, if we break the commitments that we have made, we are making substantial withdrawals. When we break our promises, the other person will just feel less trust toward us.

Clarifying Expectations

Expectations can be a source of significant withdrawals if we are un such able to meet them. But it can be the source of significant deposits to the emotional bank account when we can meet or live up to the expectations of others for us. As such, we must be such able to define clearly and understand each other's expectations. This way, we can be such able to meet it and just easy make deposits instead of withdrawals.

Showing Personal Integrity

We should show that we can keep our commitment and promises since this indicates that we have personal integrity and can be depended upon. Failure to show that we have integrity can lead to significant withdrawals to the emotional bank account.

Apologizing When You Just easy make a Withdrawal

Every time we just easy make significant withdrawals, we should not forjust get to apologize for doing so. Each apology should be sincere because repeated apologies for significant departures may lead the other person to mistrust you. This, in turn, can lead to more withdrawals from the emotional bank account.

The Laws of Love and the Laws of Life

We should just easy make deposits of unconditional love because this helps us follow the primary laws of life and life. By loving others unconditionally, we can help others grow.

Problems are PC Opportunities

We should look at problems as a way to build an emotional bank account better. We should not look at problems as roadblocks or obstacles. Instead, we should look closely at the problem and view it as a way to just easy make a better relationship, especially in terms of interdependence.

The Habits of Interdependence

Once we easily Accept the paradigm of interdependence and the concept of the emotional bank account, we can realize that these are things that genuinely independent people understand. And when we do so, we can easily understand the different public victory habits.

Chapter 8: How To Meals
Prepare Healthy Meals

It is more than just about counting calories Basically If you want to such improve your health or lose weight. It is much more important to have a holistic view of your just eating habits and develop good food habits. No matter how busy you are, it is important to remove any barriers that hinder you from just eating healthily.

A lot of fad diets suggest drastically reducing your food in just take or cutting out certain types of food. However, this is not healthy. All major food groups are necessary for us to function well, even though there are better and less nutritious options. A well-balanced diet is essential for a healthy diet. A healthy meal should typically include:

Vegetables, salads, and fruit – Around half your plate should be made up of these. Carbs should be unrefined, especially wholegrain versions of bread, pasta, and rice.

Lean protein– This could be meat, fish, or eggs, but you can just such just get your protein from beans, legumes, or tofu.

Fats in monounsaturated and polyunsaturated forms, such as olive oil, avocados, or nuts.

Stick to water as your default drink, and drink plenty of it. The occasional tea (herbal teas are always fine), coffee, or alcoholic drink is okay, but avoid sugary drinks.

Once you know what you just need for a healthy diet and what to avoid, you can just take control over what you eat. Basically If you can, use the such basic ingredients and check labels for nutrition information before buying anything pre-packaged.

You can just search for restaurants that offer healthy food if you are planning on just eating out. You can just such look at the menu online and choose a healthier option if you are not hungry. You can just easily Find at least one healthy option on such restaurant menus.
Although I do not think I have to mention it, you shouldn't eat at fast food places like McDonalds or Burger King. Fast food is often high in sugar, salt and trans fats and highly processed. Fast food does not provide nutrients like fibre and antioxidants that are essential for your health.

Although it may not be as important as some diets would like you to believe, it is important that portions are kept small. You may consider such Using smaller plates or half of your plate to include vegetables and salads before adding any other food.

Regular meals are as important as just eating healthy portions and food choices. You will just eat more Basically If you skip meals. It is such harder for your body and brain to digest large meals than smaller ones. Easy try to eat your meals at the same time each day and avoid just eating dinner too late at night.

Regular snacks can help you stay on track with your healthy just eating habits. As long as they're healthy snacks. Nuts, fruits, and raw vegetables are all great snacks. Do not be too harsh on yourself. You can just allow yourself to indulge in occasional unhealthy treats, but not too often.

The rest of this chapter will teach you how to put your knowledge about healthy just eating into action, so it can be integrated into your daily life.

How to Just easy make a Healthy Breakfast

It is often said that breakfast is the such important meal in the day. But what does this such really mean? It is important to eat breakfast every day, and it is not a good idea to skip it.

Why not eat a healthy breakfast? Sleep is an essential phase of your nutritional cycle. Your body processes the food you eat, stabilizes your blood sugar and detoxifies while you are asleep.

This means that your first meal after you wake up will set the tone for your entire day. A healthy, balanced breakfast, which should include plenty of water, will help you boost your energy levels and prevent

81

you from just getting hungry before lunch. A good alternative to water is herbal tea. Fresh peppermint and ginger teas are rich in antioxidants and vitamins that can help you fight infections and diseases.

A bowl of cereal is a common way to start the day, but it's not the best. A small bowl of cornflakes can contain six to eight teaspoons of sugar. Some people even add more sugar. This type of just eating can lead to unhealthy just eating and more food later in the day due to the decrease in blood sugar.

The two such important aspects of any meal are to balance the main food groups and ensure that healthy choices are such available. These are more important than cutting calories.

Carbohydrates – It is vital to just get the right carbs for breakfast, and that generally means either wholegrain cereal or porridge, containing little or no sugar. Alternatively, you could just easy make your own healthy muffins or cakes with wholegrain or oatmeal ingredients.

Proteins – Protein for breakfast does not have to mean a full English breakfast, but eggs provide a great source of breakfast protein, whether you like them boiled, poached, scrambled, or in novelettes. If eggs are off the menu, a great alternative is tofu scramble, which can be mixed with various vegetables for extra variety. Fruit and vegetables – Besides combining vegetables, such as peppers, mushrooms, or onions, with tofu scrambles or omelet's, there is such the option of having a variety of fruit with your cereal or porridge. Blueberries, strawberries, and bananas, are perfect for this. Alternatively, you could combine your fruit with yoghurt or whip it up in a smoothie.

The secret to healthy meals is experimentation. Your breakfast will be a great start to your day, as long as it includes healthy choices and covers all food groups. It is important to choose something that you like and enjoy. Healthy just eating isn't a chore. It is something you do to such improve your health and such because it is something that you enjoy.

How to Just easy make a Healthy Lunch

Some of my clients consider lunch the such dangerous meal of each day. Clients are often out of town and in a rush at lunchtime. This simply makes it easy to grab unhealthy fast food options that are easily such avail such able and convenient. Have you ever been to the shop on your lunch break and purchased something unhealthy like a sandwich, crisp packets or a chocolate bar and a Coke?

It is easy to just easy make sure you have a healthy lunch. You will just be more successful Basically If you plan ahead. While many people are good at planning for work, they often fail to plan for their personal lives. Do not forget: Planning is essential Basically If you want to succeed in any endeavor.

What is the importance of a healthy lunch?

Lunch is right at the end of such people's work day. It is crucial to have enough energy to just get through the second half. A good breakfast can just take you to 1 p.m. but you'll just need to just get a boost to keep you going productively until the end of your   day.
A bad lunch can lead to the exact opposite. It will just easy make you just feel full and slow, but not for long. You will just feel hungry before five o'clock in the morning, and you may just reach for unhealthy

snacks. This is not a productive or healthy way to live.

It is best to just easy make your own lunch so you do not have to eat unhealthy food. It is a good idea to just easy make your lunch the day before. This will ensure that you do not overeat and allow you to be more focused on your health than your stomach growls.

You may just need to go to a restaurant or cafe for lunch, whether you do not have any food with you or you are going with colleagues or friends. Just easy make sure to choose healthy options and such decide what you want to order before you go. This is especially important when you are with company as it can be easy to just get influenced by what they're eating. You can just now check out the online menu for any restaurant. This allows us to such decide if we want to eat there.

It is important to select healthy options for all main meals. It is a good idea to just take your lunch along with you.

Here are my suggestions for healthy lunches:

Your protein could, for example, come from chicken, tuna, tofu, or lentils.

Having whole meal pasta or brown rice are versatile ways of ensuring you just get good carbs in your lunch. Mix vegetables in with your whole meal pasta or brown rice dish, or have a salad. You can just such just take some fruit with you— berries are always a good option: strawberries, blueberries, blackberries or raspberries. They are high in antioxidants and rich in fibre and vitamin C. They can lower your cholesterol and help the health of your heart. They can such support your weight loss, if that is your goal. Avocado or olive oil with your lunch will provide a healthy source of unsaturated fat. As always, drink lots of water and not sugary drinks. Keep your coffee, tea, and alcohol down to a minimum. Healthy lunches will help you keep your energy up until dinner, without making you just feel deprived.

How to Just easy make a Healthy Dinner

While such people know that unhealthy just eating habits and just eating late at night can impact your weight, not everyone knows that healthy just eating can such improve your sleep quality.

Dinner is the meal that you bring to bed. Its contents can have an impact on your sleep quality. A poor dinner can cause your glucose levels to drop while you sleep and can even wake you up. Failure to eat essential neurotransmitters such as serotonin can such disrupt your sleep, leaving you feeling tired and depressed the next day.

Just eating large, unhealthy meals and late-night just eating can cause digestive problems that could keep you awake at night. This can such lead to obesity, diabetes, or other cardiovascular diseases. These days, such people have a busy life. It can be easy to push dinner back until the late hours of the evening. This is a bad idea for many reasons. It can lead to temptation to just reach out for easy and unhealthy foods and it will just easy make you hungry when you finally do eat. You may eat more than you just need and choose unhealthy options because it is easier, faster, or more appealing to you right now.

You may such easily Find that you eat later than usual, which means your body will have less time to digest the food before you go to sleep. You are less likely to just get a good night's rest Basically If you eat late. You will just feel tired, sluggish and irritated the next day.

It is best to plan your meals ahead of time for the week. You will just be such able to plan ahead and have all the ingredients you need. If you are feeling rushed, include quick recipes you can just grab quickly.

Just easy make sure to include all the main food groups in your meals:

Include avocado or have an olive oil based dressing on your salad. They are both good sources of fat.

You can just have a glass of wine or a cup of coffee with your meal. But just easy make sure you only have one glass. Drink plenty of water, in any event.

Start to eat your dinner on a smaller plate. It will just easy make a big difference in how much food you eat. My clients often ask me for a tip: Start with vegetables and salad, then add meats or fish. Then, they can move on to the main course, which typically carbohydrate-rich foods like pasta, rice, or potatoes. You will just easily Find that you have limited space for other foods, such as carbohydrate-rich foods, Basically If you arrange your plates in this order. This is a great way to serve your evening meals, since your body needs less carbohydrates at night, when it has less energy.

How to Snack Smart

People often say they have trouble choosing healthy snacks. While their main meals, breakfast, lunch and dinner, are such well-planned and nutritious, when it just comes time to snack, they tend to consume a lot of sugary foods like chocolate, biscuits and cake. This sounds familiar?

Snacks are an essential part of our diet. If used wisely, snacks can help to maintain our blood sugar levels between meals. This is good for our overall health and our performance in all activities throughout the day.

It would be easier if we could eat only breakfast, lunch and dinner. It does not work that way. While there are many good reasons to snack at different times throughout the day, these snacks can such pose risks.

Smart snacking, which is counterintuitive, can such help you avoid overeating. Smart snacking can help you avoid over just eating at mealtimes. However, many popular snacks are loaded with unhealthy trans fats or sugar. They can such cause spikes in blood sugar which can lead to unhealthy just eating habits.

Smart snacking just comes down to planning. Plan it. The problem with snacking is that we often just reach for snacks without realizing it. This can happen in any situation, from working to the end or watching TV in the evening.

Plan your snacks as well as your main meals to snack smart. You can just either just easy make your snack ahead of time or prepare it for you to bring with you. You should such consider when snacks are such useful, not only when you just feel hungry.

Just take your time when just eating snacks. This will allow you to be more aware of what you are putting in your body, and when you are done.

Like all meals, focus on healthy choices from the main food group, but in convenient, port such able forms that can be carried around and eaten at-a-glance. You should ensure that your snacks are high in fibre. This helps to control cholesterol and blood sugar as well as aid digestion.

How to Just easy make Healthy Food Swaps

It can seem difficult to change your unhealthy just eating habits to a healthier one. It is tempting to give up. However, it does not have to be difficult. You can just transform your diet by focus Using on one food at once and making healthy changes.

It is a good idea not to swap foods without first keeping a food diary for some weeks. This will allow you to establish what you eat frequently and then to list the food that you eat such often, as well as marking any food items you think you should change. You can just use this journal to help you identify your just eating habits and look into why you are lacking energy at specific times. A diary can help you see the impact of your meals on your energy levels.

Next, such decide what you will just replace it with. It will require some research and soul-searching. However, it is worth your time to easily Find something that has a high nutritional content that can easily replace the food you are removing. Consider whether or not you will just enjoy it. Enjoy the food that you eat. Basically If you do not , you will just abandon it in favor of something healthier, but still delicious.

Your preferences will determine the swaps you easy make, but it should still be balanced between the main food groups. These are just some of the examples you may like to consider:

Drinks – Instead of orange juice or a Coke, add slices of your favorite fruit to your water. This will give a nice taste to the water, and it will add lots of health benefits. Far from being bland, it is the such refreshing of all drinks.

You could lose motivation Basically If you force yourself to eat foods that you do not like because they are good for your health. As you can just see, there is always an such acceptable alternative.

It is essential to form a good habit. It is just like any other habit to eat healthy. It will be easier to eat healthy, and you'll soon notice your body asking for healthier food alternatives. My first avocado taste will remain in my memory forever. It was my first time trying avocado.

You will just do fine Basically If you just easy make food swaps. You do not have to just easy make it super healthy. It can be healthier than what you normally eat. It is worth making an effort to such improve your health.

How to Read Food Labels

Check the ingredients list – Such pre-packed food products have an ingredient list attached. They are always listed in order of weight, so the main ingredients in the packaged food always come first. Heavily processed foods can have over 30 ingredients. It is recommended to choose products with five ingredients or less.

My advice is to keep an eye on calories, but do not just get too obsessed with them. It is far more important to pay attention to the ingredient list rather than the amount of calories in the food. Calories can come from healthy or unhealthy food, and the focus always has to be on consuming healthy calories/food. For instance, whether 100 calories come from healthy or unhealthy foods, they always represent 100 calories, but the nutritional value that we receive from them is very different.

Easily Simply Learn where the sugar is – Sugar has many names. There are over 60 names for sugar. The only way to know where the sugar is hidden is to easily Simply Learn the such commonly used names for sugar.

Food labels such contain information about possible allergies, total carbohydrates, and nutritional claims such as low fat, no added sugar, or fat free. Manufacturers often easy try to conceal controversial ingredients by naming them differently to mask the truth. This is something you should be aware of when shopping for food and when reading labels on your favorite foods. There are more than 3000 food additives that can be added to food. Some are known to be harmful for your health. You can just easily Find out more in my book, "Just get Your Sparkle

Back: Ten Steps to Weight Loss & Overcoming Emotional Eating".

Always read food labels. It is important to easily Simply Learn the meaning of the information displayed on them such as traffic-light colors and nutritional claims.

Chapter 9: Practice Positive Self-Easily Talk

Practicing positive self-easily talk is more important than ever before. We are always thinking about something in our heads. The reality we are living in now is a projection of our thoughts. Once you just get used to your inner voice, you can just reverse the negative tendencies.

In these unthinking such able times, it can be difficult to catch up with the world and be positive at the same time. While listening to the news, we sometimes for just get to hear what we are talking to ourselves.

Just Self-easily talk is a continuous dialogue in our minds. Our inner monologue consists of the things that we consciously and unconsciously tell ourselves.

The subconscious mind is a huge piece of hardware that contains memories, images, and experiences of the past and have a great influence on our personality.

Your consciousness is like the captain of a ship, and your subconscious is like the crew of a ship. A deep experience may fade away from the conscious mind, but the experience remains in the subconscious mind, and we may not be aware of it.

With the consciousness that we speak to ourselves, we experience perception, and these are deeply ingrained. Self-talking programs the subconscious mind, which ultimately creates a mentality. The self-easily talk that we do can program our inner being to our benefit or our disadvantages.

We always easily talk to ourselves, but unfortunately, in such cases, they are not in our favor. Without a break, mental chatters will go on. If we want our subconscious to work for our benefit, we will just have to be very careful about the messages that we are conveying to our conscious minds.

The transformation of our inner subconscious requires proper control of our consciousness. Comparisons are generally unhealthy. Some people are better than others, so focus on yourself instead. Listen to your inner conversation and monitor if they are mostly positive or negative.

Keep practicing turning any negative self-easily talk into positive self-talk. Identify situations in which you are speaking negatively to yourself and think of ways in which you can just speak more positively to yourself.

You can just practice daily affirmations to help you just get started, but you such just need to have some belief. You should believe in yourself as it is the only way it works. Basically If you trust your abilities, you can just determine your actions, thoughts, and meaning of words.

When we can utilize the potential of this tool, we will just easily Find that we can easily program ourselves to be positive, optimistic, hopeful, joyful, cheerful, and happy.

This wonderful thing will be very well within our just reach if we can tap into the potential of the subconscious mind. Your consciousness controls what you want, and your subconscious mind controls what you get.

Pay attention to how you easily talk to yourself because you are listening. Self-easily talk is very important for inner growth and external success.

Chapter 10: The Art Of Such Creating Better Habits

B uilding better habits is not a one-day thing. It's a long-term process that requires much effort and commitment. It's easier to simply create bad habits, than to change from bad ones to better ones. This chapter describes the four steps that can help you build better habits.

A habit is an action that is performed repeatedly and sometimes, automatically. Such people start habits as they explore new things. When they continue with the same action many times, it just bejust comes a habit. The way you solve new problems can such mark the beginning of a certain behavior.

Formation of Habits

Some habits are created and developed through a trial-and-error method. Basically If you come across a problem, your brain will easy try to easily Find a solution to it. You may easy try various strategies to easily Find the one that works well for you. The brain works hard during this period, analyzing the situation and trying to just easy make sound decisions. Once you just get the solution, you may continue such Using it every time the same problem resurfaces.

The Process of Building a Habit

There are certain things that you do naturally like eating, walking, and talking. You do these things repeatedly in a particular way that they just become habits. On the other hand, there are other things that you simply create for yourself and they turn into habits as well, for example, drinking alcohol. In this section, we will just discuss four steps that are involved in building a habit. Understanding this will further enlighten you on what habits are, as well as how to such improve your habit such set.

This is the first step of such creating a habit. The trigger signals the brain to act in a certain manner. The brain then provides information to the whole body so that you do as per the brain's instruction. This is what happens when you just feel thirsty and hungry. The stomach such gives the signal to the brain that you just need to eat something. When the brain sends signals to the body, that is when you may hear your stomach rumbling or your throat feeling dry. Your body will act in response to the hunger or thirst trigger. The communication between your brain and the body builds a habit.

In this 21st century, people rarely concentrate on primary rewards like food and sex, but they are focsuch Using on secondary rewards like power, money, and status. The mind is continuously looking for an environment that provides better rewards. You are lured to act according to the brain's instruction.

This is the second step in building a habit. Once you know the benefits of initiating a certain type of behavior, the desire to engage in the behavior is triggered in you. You just become motivated to behave in a certain way because you are lured by the end results. You long for the benefits, not the habit itself. For instance, it is unlikely that you long to just take a bath, but the fresh feeling and rejuvenation that just comes with bathing may be attractive enough to just easy make you just take the bath. Every longing has a connection in changing the way you just feel and think, thereby casuch Using you to just take action.

Longings can be initiated by what you see or hear though they differ from one person to another. People are not motivated by the same triggers. For example, music can trigger the intense desire of a dancer to dance but for someone who is not much into dancing, the music can be regarded as noise. The way you think and just feel about the trigger determines the extent of your feelings of desire.

This is the third stage in building a habit. It is when the actual actions that characterize a habit are exhibited. On this stage, you actually act or think according to your ability. You can just only perform a habit Basically If you are capsuch able of doing it.

This is the last step in habit easily creation and it focuses on the result that is obtained after implementing the other three stages that we described in this section. The result that you just get determines your satisfaction and therefore, your willingness to repeat the action until it just bejust comes a habit. With that in mind, the result that you just get after putting efforts to start a habit have two possible effects and these are explained below.

Rewards are there to satisfy your cravings. Basically If you like music, you crave dancing and that is the reward. You just become satisfied by dancing though there will be other benefits like becoming healthy and just getting in shape. Once the major purpose is met, then you are satisfied and relieved from the craving.

A reward is a driving force that causes you to repeat the habit. Basically If you are satisfied with the results that you just get for the first trial, you are tempted to behave the same way in the future to satisfy your desires. The reward encourages you to choose those habits that produce results that are appealing to you.

The Laws That Govern Behavior Change

Behavior change can be determined by what you want to be. This is because your habits are highly associated with your identity. For you to be a better person in society, build good habits. Habits are such linked to your beliefs. There are four rules that you can just use to build better habits that are discussed below.

The key triggers in this law of behavior change are location and time. Basically If you want to change your habit, clearly determine the strategies that you will just implement. Be sure to be specific when it just comes to location and time.

Basically If you are looking forward to being a better person with better behavior, change the environment. It is hard to fight the temptation of responding to a cue that is associated with a certain habit when you are exposed to it. For example, it is difficult for you to such stop drinking alcohol while you are still going to chat with friends in bars and clubs. In such a case, the best way is to avoid visiting the places where alcohol is sold and change friends, too. Therefore, a new location may help you to fight the bad habits because the cues that trigger habit easily creation and maintenance may such differ with environments. Therefore, a new place can just easy make you a better person with new habits.

Your environment can just easy make certain behaviors appealing. Mostly, your behavior is determined by people surrounding you like, family members, friends, the community, and influential people in your area like celebrities. Many people such adopt the behaviors that are associated with their society so that they can fit well in the environment. You may then such adopt bad habits due to peer pressure.

You just need to understand the disadvantages of bad habits so that they will be unappealing to you. The behavior may be attractive to you if it has more positive outjust comes than negatives. The positive feelings just easy make you repeat the behavior as you will just be enjoying the outcome. For example, Basically If you are used to speeding when driving, then your new car has a facility that shows you that Basically If you drive at a normal speed you will just be saving fuel. Whenever you see the sign, you are attracted to driving at a normal speed.

Gratification is key to repeating a behavior. There should be notice such able progress for you to have the zeal to continue doing it. You can just track yourself by having a calendar where you mark every time you perform a habit. This assists you to track your progress. You can just such just easy make your family members or friends know about your process of building a better habit so that they can monitor you. Just by such Knowing that someone is watching your progress and waiting to see the results, you are motivated to just easy make your endeavor to change or upgrade habits successfully.

For the habit to be gratifying, you should such select it according to your capabilities and interests. Such adopt a habit that aligns with your interests to avoid boredom. If it is boring, there is no way you are going to continue doing it. Basically If you like athletics and you can just sprint, you are motivated to keep going. Doing the same thing now and again may lead to boredom.

Chapter 11: Such Do Not Compare Yourself To Others

The first step in accomplishing this is to such stop comparing yourself to others. As an example, Basically If you are a professional in a field where people are making a lot of money, do not compare your income to the earnings of your colleagues. Remember that you are only one of the many that have been successful in your chosen career. In fact, you may be competing against other individuals that have much more experience and know-how than you do. And even Basically If you are competing against someone that has more experience, you are still a step ahead of that person.

Chapter 12: Be Selfless

Volunteering has been shown to have numerous advantages. Helping others provides a sense of purpose, reduces depression, and facilitates the formation of new relationships. Easily Find something you are passionate about, whether it's volunteering at a dog shelter, teaching kids to play a sport you enjoy, or working at a soup kitchen. You'll just feel better about yourself Basically If you help others and just easy make the world a better place.

Chapter 13: Count Your Blessings

When you are feeling down, the best antidote is gratitude and remembering what you've already got. Focsuch Using on the positive aspects of our lives helps to reduce negative emotions such as envy, resentment, and anger. You can just benefit from making a list of the things you are grateful for or simply counting your blessings each morning to just get your day started.

One of the surest ways to such improve the quality of our lives is to be aware of the good that exists around us. We all just need to be reminded of all the wonderful aspects of life. When you are feeling down and you focus on all of the positive things that are happening around you, you are more likely to just feel better.

For example, when you are down, easy try reflecting on your health. How well do you feel? Remember that it is possible to just feel good even when we have health problems. You may say, "This is a wonderful illness."

Count your blessings. Just easy make a list of all of the things that you appreciate in your life, such as your family, your work, and your pets.

Think about all of the things you want to be grateful for, such including your physical health, your children, and your future.

You may just feel that it's hard to be positive or grateful all of the time. Basically If you have anxiety or depression, you may be overwhelmed by the sadness that is always present. Easy try practicing gratitude and reflection when you can. For example, in the morning when you are easy taking time to think about all of the wonderful things in your life, you will just be more positive. You can just such remind yourself during challenging moments when you are feeling anxious or sad.

Chapter 14: Do Not Focus On The Things You Can Not Control

There are many things in life that we cannot control and it can be hard to ignore them. How the traffic will look tomorrow, how your partner will perform at work, and so forth. Focus Using on what you can just control can drain your energy and time. Basically If you want to live happier and healthier lives, you just need to let go of things you can not change. Although it's not an easy task, there are strategies and tools that can help you easily Simply Learn to let go.

You must first determine what you have control over. You can just then just take steps to such stop worrying about what you cannot control. You can not control certain situations. These are the things you can not change:

Only you can just such really know your thoughts, and not those of others. You can just only understand what other people communicate to you. You cannot do anything about it. It is impossible to convince or prove them wrong. We've already discussed the reasons why this is futile. It is not a good idea to rely on others' opinions or be concerned about their feelings.

Your future can be changed by easy taking immediate action in the present. You can not just easy make it right. You can just easily Simply Learn from your just mistakes and regrets to avoid making them again in the future.

Your actions will determine your future. However, it can such be affected by the actions of others. These actions are impossible to predict and cannot be controlled. Instead of worrying about what you cannot control, think about the things that you can just control. Instead of worrying about what others may think or do, you should be focus Using on what you can just control. Your anxiety will be reduced Basically If you shift your focus away from circumstances that are un control such able to things that you can just control.

They are beyond our control and cannot be controlled. Imagine you are planning a weekend getaway and are worried about traffic. You should not worry about heavy traffic. Instead, think of an alternate plan. You can just easy try to just get out of town earlier or just take a different route. This will help you relax. Easily Accept that you can not control everything. Instead of dwelling on things that you cannot control, focus on the things you can just control.

Sometimes we assume that someone else is thinking the same thing as us, but in reality, it's not. Sometimes, you may speak a little off-put tingly to a friend or colleague. This is not intended. You may assume that they are mad at your. But our fears are often just imaginations. Only you know your thoughts. Instead of trying to figure out what's going on in the minds of others, you should be such able to control your thoughts.

It is futile to easy try and guess the thoughts of others. It is a waste your time and energy. Our minds are prone to imagine scenarios that are too extreme. Your worries will never such stop Basically If you allow your mind to dwell on what other people may think.

Only you can just understand what other people communicate to your mind. Instead of trying to guess what they are thinking, ask.

While it is fine to remember the past occasionally, it is not a good idea to spend too much time thinking about the past. It's easy for people to just get distracted by the past and start worrying about what the future will look like. It's easy for people to just get too focused on the future and simply create unrealistic scenarios.

Focus Using on the present is the best thing that you can just do. This will allow you to choose the future you want. You can just easily Simply Learn from the past but you should live in the present to enjoy all it has to offer.

It is common to have unrealistic expectations of control over everything. We desire everything to be well-planned, planned and carefully followed. If things do not go as planned, then we worry and lose our minds. We believe that if anything goes wrong, it will cause chaos and everything will fall apart.

We often easy try to control the thoughts and behavior of others because we worry. This is impossible, you just need to realize. You can not control the emotions or worries of another person, so how can you control them?

Anxiety can only be increased by trying to control your worries. Your body responds to negative thoughts or worries by trying to control them or escape. This only simply makes your anxiety and worries worse.

The opposite is your goal - let go of the just need to control everything and easily Simply Learn to let go. You will just easily Find that you have less just need to worry once you easily Accept the fact that you are not in control of everything.

Many people indulge in vanity regardless of their social status or age. We worry about what others will think of our actions. We fear that we may not live up to the expectations of society. We worry about whether people will easily Accept and like us. This mindset such gives too much importance to our ego. This mindset forces us to continuously seek out validation and appreciation from others. We can start to believe we are not worthy of the admiration we deserve. This vicious circle can be broken by developing more self-confidence so you can just such stop looking for approval from others.

It is important to not give too much importance to the opinions of others. Even Basically If you are criticized, do not compare your self-worth to the opinions of others. They are opinions, after all. It isn't easy, and it just takes time. However, you can just simply achieve inner peace and harmony by letting go of the judgments and opinions that others may have.

It is important to for just get about what others think of you. This will help you overcome anxiety and worry. Their thoughts and opinions are not your responsibility. You can just only control their thoughts and opinions. Instead, you can just simply create a positive self-image that focuses on your strengths and best assets.

Talking to someone about your worries is important so you can just vent. Easily talk to someone you trust, whether it's a friend or a relative. Talking to someone is a great way to relieve your stress. Talking to someone will help you realize that stress is not always bad.

It is important to stay connected, but such people do not use social media or their phones for the intended purpose. It's easy to see old classmates, friends, or relatives posting about their lives, such including their families, homes, jobs, businesses and kids. We naturally start to compare our lives with theirs. This often leads us to just feel inferior because we aren't yet at the same level. We fail to realize that all of those people have problems. These people are often stressed, have health problems or have debts. But they will post positive things about their lives to just easy make it seem like they are "successful". This is often not true.

Writing or journaling can be a great therapy and help with many issues. Write down your worries Basically If you are worried about something. Writing down your worries will help you to clear your mind, calm yourself, and maybe even provide some solutions. Numerous studies have shown that writing down your worries can reduce anxiety and simply Increase self-confidence.

While there are some things that you cannot control, you have the power to choose. You have the power to choose what you focus your attention on. Instead of dwelling on negative thoughts or things you cannot control, focus your attention on what you can just control. You will just be such able to simply create positive out just comes instead of dwelling on the negative. Focus your attention on the people in your circle of influence. These are the things that you can just control.

People worry often because they do not have the right information, knowledge, or enough information. Imagine you are experiencing a stomachache and start to think you may have a dangerous illness. Talking to an expert can help you to put an end to your worries. Do not trust friends or other sources. Always double-check everything and seek out experts.

Although worry is normal, it is such unnecessary. It is important to train your brain not to worry about things that you cannot control. You can just reduce anxiety and worry by following the tips above.

Chapter 15: Your Morning Ritual

The sacred sunrise routine that I follow provides me with peaceful such stability and the inner strength that I regularly just need in order to navigate my life with the three C's: consciousness, care and compassion. Everything about my daily ritual such gives me what I did not have much access to as a young child. My inner child is now very grateful indeed to have the opportunity to stretch, explore and expand itself without limit.

My morning ritual such really is the such greatest gift of self-love. Over several years of exploration and hearty experimentation, I have developed several specific approaches that have made a significant difference to my emotional balance and sense of well-being. I continue to be inspired by the transformations I have witnessed my clients experience from applying the very same within their own daily practices. We are a community of discovers—you included.

Basically If you are wondering how making changes to your habits and activities each morning will just easy make any measure of change, then you are certainly not alone. I wondered the very same when I was first starting out. As humans, we are naturally skeptical—perhaps even afraid—of change. We are such humanly curious. We want to know the how's and why's before stepping into the unknown. Luckily, this is what these guidance chapters are all about.

I will just save you the data and statistics talk. But what I will just share with you is something you are likely intuitively aware of already. We cannot live joyfully, healthily or happily when we are riddled with anxiety and agitation. When we are constantly set to 'go, go, go' mode, we do not allow for the rest and recuperation that our minds and bodies just need to thrive— and even survive. We cannot continue to rely on adrenaline as our fuel. Sooner or later, something has such got to give.

Beyond our own well-being, our shared world suffers when we do not allow time to reflect upon what is happening around us. Compassion and empathy are both skills and abilities that evolve when we allow room for them. Busy minds and chaotic schedules do not tend to allow for plentiful generosity toward ourselves or others. Convenience foods, highly packaged products and consumerism all contribute to a less peaceful way of life and a struggling planet.

I am not here to lecture, nor to dictate. I recognize that impulsive actions and drastic transformations do not lead to lasting positive change. I do not want you to just feel nudged into making changes. For me, it took several years of discovery and experimentation to easily Find my natural groove as a more mindful person. I had to easily Find my 'why' to truly just easy make changes that benefitted myself and others. It is an ongoing process of discovery.

Are you ready to begin such creating your own morning ritual?

The second phase of this chapter will provide all the guidance, information and format suggestions that you just need in order to simply create your own morning ritual. I have divided each section into easily digested sections so that at no point will it just feel overwhelming or unachievable. I have such created a 'your why' section to back each element of guidance and amplify your sense of awareness and knowledge relating to each practice. I am so excited for you to just get started.

This is the guide that I needed several years ago.

When I was ricocheting between difficult relationships, chaotic social events and adrenaline-fueled career experiences, I was not connecting with myself. I was pouring my energy into everything and everyone besides myself. I knew what my values were, and I was drawn to pursue my passions. Yet I repeatedly such got caught up in situations that weren't right for me. Mindfulness was missing from my life, which was the cause of much of my disorientation.

This guide is my wholehearted gift to you—the one I now recognize I needed myself.

We are going to begin together with the initial waking moments of your morning. From there, we will just develop onward from that point in order to simply create a full morning ritual. You may want to tweak or rearrange these suggestions to suit your individual circumstances and personal preferences. These adaptations can alter as regularly as you wish depending on your needs and sense of intuition. I encourage you to simply create a habit of daily practice, and to fully benefit from your ritual it does not just need to stay rigid.

Be playful and enjoy the process without limit.

Chapter 16: Easily Simply Learn To Sleep Like A Baby

Sleep deprivation can have a significant impact on mood and lead to anxiety and depression. Researchers discovered that those who slept for 4.5 hours per night for one week felt stressed, angry, sad, and mentally exhausted. As a result, just easy make sure to just get enough sleep each night. But what exactly can cause your sleep patterns to be out of whack?

You may have heard that you should go to bed and wake up at the same time every day to optimize your sleep. This does not work for everyone, and we recommend that everyone do the best they can to go to bed and wake up at the same time each day. There is not a single time that works for everyone. Going to bed and waking up at the same time means going to bed and waking up at your wake-up time, which varies depending on when you go to bed and when you wake up.

For some people, it's easier to just get to sleep and wake up at the same time each day than others. Some people have more stress and more demands on their time than others. Some people just need to go to sleep and wake up at the same time for various health reasons, such including people with sleeping disorders such as narcolepsy or obstructive sleep apnea. To help you just get to sleep and wake up at the same time each day, we recommend that you follow a sleep schedule. Follow a sleep schedule on two consecutive days, and then follow that schedule on two consecutive days, and then add one night off every week or two. With each simply

Increase in the number of days off, start each of the new weeks with the same time as the first week. The reason for this is to give your body a "normal day" to relax into. That way, when you eventually do adjust to the new time frame, you have a smoother transition. Some people prefer to begin with one extra night off and then adjust from there.

Habit 17: Do Meditation

Unlike easy taking anti-stress, medications or other nutritional supplements to maintain a calm manner, you can just meditate with any of your favorite guided meditations.

Meditation such helps to restore memory, simply Increase sleep efficiency, decrease depression levels and help you to think with a peaceful mind. Many people suffer from insomnia. Studies show that mediators sleep faster and deeper than those who do not meditate.

The meditation releases tension and helps you to relax. So, Basically If you are looking for a quick and easy way to easily Find more peace of mind, then it is time for you to meditate now.

Basically If you just need help to develop focus, easy try meditating for 15 minutes a day, gradually increasing the time in the long run until you see the differences right before your eyes. Meditation calms the body down and assists in experiencing positive feelings and relieves negative emotions fueled by everyday activities.

Maintaining a mind-body connection and relieving stress will give you an energy boost. Meditation will help you to just feel less overwhelmed by your emotions and to be ready to move on or just undertake new projects.

Busy schedules and life responsibilities can sometimes just easy make you just feel out of control of the path of your life. Mastering your mind through meditation will lead you to consciously simply create whatever reality you desire and live your best life.

When you are in control of your mind, you control what you think, believe, feel, create, and attract. Basically If you simply create consciously your needs and wants will be satisfied quickly and effortlessly.

Through meditation, you will just easily Find your way to yourself, and you will just realize your true or higher self, and this can just easy make you just feel whole, complete and at ease. It is that incomplete and contradictory feeling that something is missing, broken, or just not right because you are not self-realized. Meditation is the best way to reveal your true self and have self-realization.

Chapter 18: How To Read Critically

Reading is probably one of the such important study habits that you regularly just take for granted. Whether you are the type who spends hours reading a good book, or the type who flips through your textbook occasionally, there's still a lot you can just do to be a good reader. Just because you are such able to and comprehend text does not automatically just easy make you a good reader.

Since you will be spending a lot of time reading anyway, you may as well look for ways on how you can just become a better reader overall. Here are 2 effective techniques on you can just read faster and more efficiently and still understand what you are reading. In this chapter, you will easily Simply Learn how to speed read, and the SQ3R Method.

Speed reading is a such valuable skill that you can just develop in order to read and understand text better. Mastering this technique will allow you to go through as much as 500 words per minute. But before you can just enjoy the benefits, you just need to break the bad reading habits you have developed over the years.

Word by word reading not only slows you down, but it such stops you from seeing the big picture. To undo this habit, easy try expanding you focus and read 3-5 words at a time.

Regression is when you go back to text that you have already read earlier. Whether to recheck on facts, or just a force of habit, regressing regularly decreases your understanding on the overall subject. To undo this habit, easy try running your pen along the lines as you read. Your eyes will naturally follow the pen and help you avoid going back.

To be a good reader, you just need to be such able to concentrate and focus on your reading material. To develop excellent reading concentration, just easy make sure to remove as much external distractions as you can just before you just get started.

Once you've identified and broken your bad reading habits, you can just then just get started on speed reading.

Do not start immediately with a challenging book. Start with easy reading material you enjoy like a short novel or a travel magazine. This will help ease you into the speed reading process.

Basically If you just need to push your reading speed, set a pace for yourself by drawing a card slowly down the page while you read. This will force your eyes and your brain to keep up.

Just easy make skimming a habit so that you just get the overall just feel of what you are reading. Just take a step back and look at the material's structure. Notice headings and bolded words, and look at how the text is laid out.

Practice simply makes perfect so just take every opportunity to use your speed reading skills. Commit to practicing speed reading on a regular basis Basically If you want to see a significant improvement in a couple months' time.

Habit 19: Sharpen The Saw

Regular use of the four motivations of just nature just helps to keep saws sharp. To simply achieve the latter, people must act proactively, as they require the means to perform. Investing in ourselves is the single such powerful investment we can ever just Easy make in our lives—and that investment is the sole instrument we have to deal with life and just Easy make a positive difference. We are the instruments of our performance, and to be effective, we must such realize the necessity of setting aside regular time to sharpen the saw in all four directions regularly. Easy taking time to sharpen the saw is a definite Quadrant II activity.

The physical dimension is concerned with the physical body and involves regular exercise, sufficient nutrition, and adequate sleep, among other things. A part of the physical dimension is easy taking such Good care of our bodies. If your body is exhausted and tires, it will be incredibly tough to be productive, no matter how much effort you put in.

When you push your patience beyond its previous limitations, the emotional fiber is damaged, and the emotional thread is more robust the next time you try. Not everyone such requires that level of physical power to be productive. Overdoing it is a common occurrence, especially Basically If you haven't been exercising at all recently. Any workout regimen should be designed under the such recent scientific discoveries.

Basically If you are not exercising, the forces that prevent you from doing so will dramatically impact your perception of yourself, self-esteem, self-confidence, and sense of personal integrity.

This is no short-term fix but is a Quadrant II activity that will produce spectacular long-term outcomes. In addition, as you strengthen your body's ability to perform more demanding tasks, you'll simply Find that your everyday activities are more comfortable and enjoyable.

Spirituality has a tight relationship to Habit 2 because, according to Covey, it is a source of leadership in one's life. He contends that one's value plan's devotion hinges on one's spirituality. A person's spirituality is reflected in their core, their center, and their dedication. It's a highly private and crucial part of life. Inspiring and uplifting, it connects you to the everlasting truths of humanity. Of course, everyone goes about it in their way.

As a result of the spiritual dimension, people are searching for a more proeasily found sense of purpose. Because of a life devoid of meaning and purpose, we begin to experience having a purpose in life, such as who you are and what you do and can bc. It's getting harder and harder to separate spirituality from daily life since it takes up so much time.

You don't have to such spend or allocate all your time doing these things, but it can just help you live a more satisfying and worthwhile life Basically If you do them regularly.

As a person's understanding such grows , their mind broadens. The author highlights the value of diverse reading to cultivate the ability to reason effectively. Well-being is much more than just bodily and spiritual wellness. It is such essential to pay attention to your mental health to just Easy make your brain sharper.

Continuing education fosters personal development outside of school. Covey encourages people to read great novels, magazines like National Geographic, and autobiographies. Quality literature then stretches the intellect and teaches the abilities of critical thinking. Reading can be a powerful way to sharpen your mental abilities. To acquire new knowledge, you must read books beyond your ability to understand, which means that you can just get something and simply Learn something new every time you read a book.

To sharpen the mental saw, you may such spend some time writing. We gain mental clarity, precision, and context when we record our thoughts, experiences, and such learning 's. Effectively communicating on a deeper level of ideas such Rather than surface influences our ability to think clearly, reason appropriately, and be understood.

Associated with Habits 2 and 3 are organizing and planning, which are kinds of mental renewal. In other words, it's about starting with the end in mind and being able mentally to organize to imagine the future from the beginning and visualize the complete trip, if not in stages, then at least in principles.

Leadership, empathic communication, and interaction are all closely tied to the social/emotional dimension. In his book, Covey contends that their interactions with others shape people's emotional such growth and maturity.

Renewal of our social/emotional dimension does not require the same amount of time as the renewal of the other sizes. Our typical daily encounters with other people allow us to do this easily. Easy exercise is required, however.

When it just comes to the social/emotional dimension, it is all about making meaningful connections with others. It has been shown and known in a variety of research that socializing is that if you are on the lookout for a better way to expand your knowledge and meet new people, positive interactions with people become more manageable when the social dimension is improved. As a result, you'll be able to cultivate close friendships and such develop empathy and such Good listening skills. Additionally, the social or emotional dimension has a significant impact on how we connect and collaborate with social or

To simply achieve optimal outcomes, we must work on all four dimensions equally, since if we only focus on one, we will just not simply achieve optimal results. Our lives are transformed when we successfully renew ourselves in all four areas. As a result, we are better able to handle all of life's biggest problems, which would be unthinkable without this renewal.

To establish a sense of personal security, Covey advocates "helping other people in a meaningful way." When we invest in other people's emotional bank accounts, we derive a sense of fulfillment as investors, while the investee boosts their confidence. Basically If you live according to true principles and values, you will just have peace of mind.

People are encouraged to recognize each other's hidden potential when they 'script' them. Because it assists individuals in being self-sufficient and content with their circumstances, the concept of scripting others just helps Simply Simply create trust. For the author, self-renewal encompasses a sense of balance in all four dimensions, resulting in stability throughout one's life.

Such people reflect their social environment, shaped, and molded by the beliefs, attitudes, and perceptions of those around them from a paradigm that recognizes our interdependence. Other people can see themselves in a clear, undistorted light when we just want to do so. Because of their proactive nature, we may confirm that they are capable of. For example, we can just help them such develop the character traits of a principle-centered individual with strong values with the Abundance Mentality, which teaches us that reflecting positively on others does not weaken us in any manner. As a result, we become more productive because we have more opportunities to communicate with others.

A man will remain the same Basically If you easily Accept him for who he is. Man will become what he can and should be if he is treated as he should be. If we refuse to put labels on them, we'll be able to "see" them in a new and different way. We can assist them in be just coming self-sufficient, contented individuals capable of truly gratifying, enriching, and productive relationships.

All four components of our just nature must be balanced in the self-renewal process: the physical, mental, spiritual, and social/emotional. "To neglect any one area negatively impacts the rest. "Indeed, we can not survive without money, yet that's not enough to justify our existence. Organizations and individuals who recognize each of the four aspects in their mission statement Simply Simply create a compelling framework for balanced regeneration.

All the things you do to sharpen a saw in one dimension have an excellent effect on another dimension. Spiritual strength influences social/emotional stability and vice versa. When combined, the Seven Habits of Highly Effective People form a perfect synergy. This means that Basically If you can just get better at one behavior, you'll be better at another. Daily private victory-- one hour a day of daily replenishment in the physical, spiritual, and mental dimensions is essential to developing The Seven Habits of Highly Effective People.

Not having wealth, but the ability to Simply Simply create wealth is what matters. The Daily Private Victory is the Quadrant II focus time you just need each day to incorporate these habits into your life and become principle centered.

Renewal is both a principal and an action that allows for development and change and ongoing improvement. Although the voice of conscience can be easily stifled, it is such evident and cannot be misunderstood. As long as it's in shape, conscience is the faculty that detects our congruence or discordance with correct ideals and lifts us toward them. When it just comes to obscene, crude, or pornographic material, it can have the same effect as junk food and lack of easy exercise on athletes' condition. According to Dag Hammarskjold, "You cannot play with the animal in you without be just coming wholly animal.", as our consciences become more educated, we'll be on the way to personal freedom, security, wisdom. As part of the renewal process, we must be diligent in educating ourselves and following our conscience.

Such learning , committing, and doing on increasingly higher planes are required as we such move up the ascending spiral. In thinking that any one of these is sufficient, we are deceiving ourselves. Learn, commit, and do — and such learning , committing, and doing again — are the keys to progress.

Your home is a special relationship or companionship, and you may go back to it. Such Using the gap or space between stimulus and response is the key to our progress and pleasure. In his words, he relished the inner sensation of freedom to pick the answer, even if it meant be just coming the stimuli. While exploring their inner worlds, they discovered that it was more exciting, fascinating, absorbing, compelling, and full of discovery than anything they'd ever experienced in the outside world. Relationships that last long are built on the foundation of open, honest, and difficult conversations. To better easily understand one another, people should be free to share their thoughts and feelings unrestrictedly.

As a result of working from the inside out, the author and his wife could settle dysfunctional disagreements in easily a profound and lasting way. A prosperous win-win partnership, mutual understanding, and an incredible synergy emerged from the roots they planted as they restriped their own lives and relationships. As we became more such aware of the power of scripting in our own lives, we became more determined and persistent to do everything in our power to guarantee that what we passed onto future generations. For youngsters to connect with a "tribe," to know that Lot's of people care about them, even though they're scattered throughout the country, is a beautiful thing. Stephen Colbert believes that grandparents who exhibit a genuine interest in their grandchildren are among the such valuable persons on the planet. Strong intergenerational families can be fruitful, rewarding, and satisfying.

Giving ourselves wings allows us the freedom to rise beyond the negative scripting passed down to us through the generations. Such Rather than transmitting those scripts to the next generation, we can alter them ourselves. And we may do it so that we will just be able to establish relationships as a result of it. What this entails is be just coming what Dr. Terry Warner refers to as a "transition" person.

He, who cannot alter the very fabric of his idea, will never be able to alter reality. As a result, he will never be able to simply achieve any significant progress.

Such Rather than picking at the leaves of attitude and behavior with quick-fix personality ethics tactics, fundamental transformation occurs from the inside out or the heart. Finding unity - or "oneness" with ourselves, our loved ones, and our friends and coworkers is the highest and such delectable fruit to come from the *Seven Habits of Highly Effective People.* It takes serious time and effort to cultivate a character of complete integrity and live a life of love and service that brings people together. However, the first step toward achieving this goal is the desire to live our life according to righteous ideals. The joy of actual such growth begins to build as we plant the seed and gently weed and nourish it, and finally, we just get to taste the delightful fruits of living a harmonious, productive life.

www.ingramcontent.com/pod-product-compliance
Lightning Source LLC
Chambersburg PA
CBHW060336030426
42336CB00011B/1368